A Note to Parents and Teachers

DK READERS is a compelling reading programme for children, designed in conjunction with leading literacy experts, including Cliff Moon M.Ed., Honorary Fellow of the University of Reading. Cliff Moon has spent many years as a teacher and teacher educator specializing in reading and has written more than 160 books for children and teachers. He is series editor to Collins Big Cat.

Beautiful illustrations and superb full-colour photographs combine with engaging, easy-to-read stories to offer a fresh approach to each subject in the series. Each DK READER is guaranteed to capture a child's interest while developing his or her reading skills, general knowledge, and love of reading.

The five levels of DK READERS are aimed at different reading abilities, enabling you to choose the books that are exactly right for your child:

Pre-level 1: Learning to read
Level 1: Beginning to read
Level 2: Beginning to read alone
Level 3: Reading alone
Level 4: Proficient readers

The "normal" age at which a child begins to read can be anywhere from three to eight years old. Adult participation through the lower levels is very helpful for providing encouragement, discussing storylines and sounding out unfamiliar words.

No matter which level you select, you can be sure that you are helping your child learn to read, then read to learn!

LONDON, NEW YORK, MUNICH,
MELBOURNE AND DELHI

Series Editor Deborah Lock
Managing Art Editor Rachael Foster
Art Editor Gemma Fletcher
DTP Designer Emma Hansen-Knarhoi
Production Georgina Hayworth
Picture Researcher Rob Nunn
Jacket Designer Simon Oon

Reading Consultant
Cliff Moon, M.Ed.

Published in Great Britain by
Dorling Kindersley Limited,
80 Strand, London WC2R 0RL

Copyright © 2007 Dorling Kindersley Limited
A Penguin Company

2 4 6 8 10 9 7 5 3 1
DD390 - 12/06

All rights reserved. No part of this publication may be
reproduced, stored in a retrieval system, or transmitted in
any form or by any means, electronic, mechanical,
photocopying, recording, or otherwise, without the prior
written permission of the copyright owner.

A CIP record for this book is available
from the British Library

ISBN: 978-1-40531-942-3

Colour reproduction by Colourscan, Singapore
Printed and bound in China by L Rex Printing Co., Ltd.

The publisher would like to thank the following for their kind permission
to reproduce their photographs:
(Key: a=above; b=below/bottom; c=centre; l=left; r=right; t=top)
Alamy Images: David Noble Photography 30b; Roger Hutchings 26t; Ron
Niebrugge 21; Pacific Press Service 4tl; Stock Connection Distribution 20bl;
Corbis: Rick Gomez 4b; Pete Leonard/zeta 25; James Noble 2 3t; Robert Harding
World Imagery 24; **Getty Images:** DK Stock/Christina Kennedy 5t; Iconica/Frans
Lemmens 13; The Image Bank/Peter Adams 19; Photonica/Doug Plummer 23;
naturepl.com: Atlo 17; **PunchStock:** Digital Vision 4cla; Mediaimages 28;
Photodisc Red 12; Stockbyte Platinum 5br; **Science & Society Picture Library:**
National Railway Museum 25t; **Science Photo Library:** Martin Bond 11; Robert
Brook 27; Ted Kinsman 2b, 9t; NASA 31b; US Geological Survey 31cr; Tom Van
Sant, Geosphere Project/Planetary Visions 30; **SeaPics.com:** Doc White 15;
Still Pictures: T. BALABAADKAN/UNEP 20br; Randy Brandon 26b; ullstein -
Mehrl 21t

All other images © Dorling Kindersley
For more information see: www.dkimages.com

Discover more at
www.dk.com

DK READERS

Water Everywhere

Written by Jill Atkins

A Doring Kindersley Book

We use lots of water
every day.
We have baths
and brush our teeth.

We water the garden.
We wash our dishes,
our clothes and
our cars.

We go swimming
and play water sports.

Washing hands

We wash our hands before meals so we don't get germs on our food that can make us sick.

We also need water. We have to drink water every day to keep our bodies healthy and alert.

Water is the best thing to drink between meals.

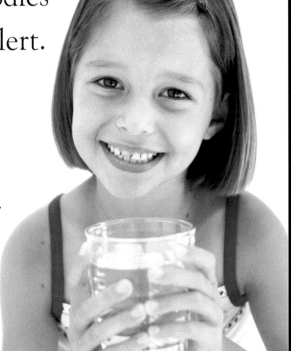

Almost three-quarters of the planet Earth is covered in water.
Most of the water is contained in five large oceans and several small seas.

Mediterranean Sea

Caribbean Sea

Sargasso Sea

ATLANTIC OCEAN

PACIFIC OCEAN

We cannot drink this water, because it is too salty. It would make us sick to drink it. So how does this water become the water we use and need?

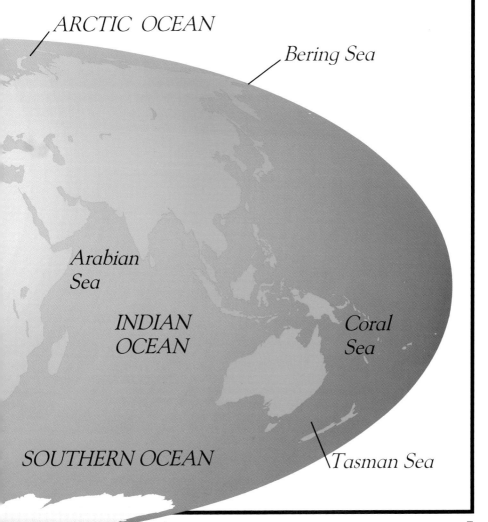

ARCTIC OCEAN

Bering Sea

Arabian Sea

INDIAN OCEAN

Coral Sea

SOUTHERN OCEAN

Tasman Sea

Water in the oceans and seas
is warmed by the sun.
The heated water becomes
droplets that rise up and
form clouds.
The wind blows the clouds
over the land.
Then the water cools and falls
from the clouds as rain.
Rainwater is called freshwater
because it is no longer salty.
Some rainwater runs
into rivers, which
flow into lakes or
back into the sea.

Snowflakes

In cold weather, water from clouds falls as sleet, hail or snow. Each snowflake has a different pattern with six points.

This process is called the water cycle.

Our water comes from lakes
or natural springs under the ground.
It is cleaned so that it is safe to drink.
Underground pipes carry the water
into our homes.

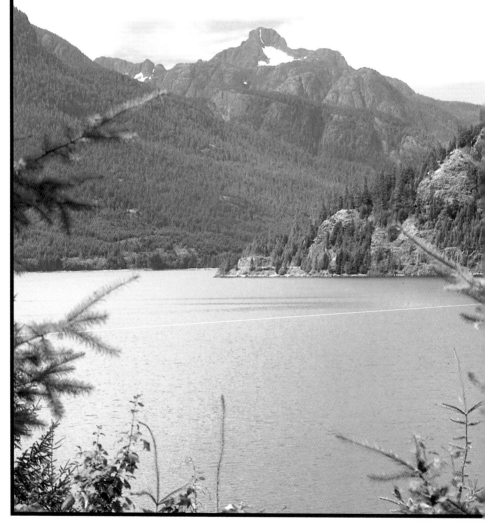

Storing water

Sometimes a dam is built across a river to make a reservoir. Some of the water we use is stored there.

It is important that we try not to waste water. Adults can help save water by fixing leaky pipes. You can help by remembering to turn off taps.

Animals also need water
for drinking and bathing.
Elephants can suck more than
7.5 litres (two gallons) of water
into their long trunks.
They squirt this water
into their mouths to drink
or over their backs to keep cool.

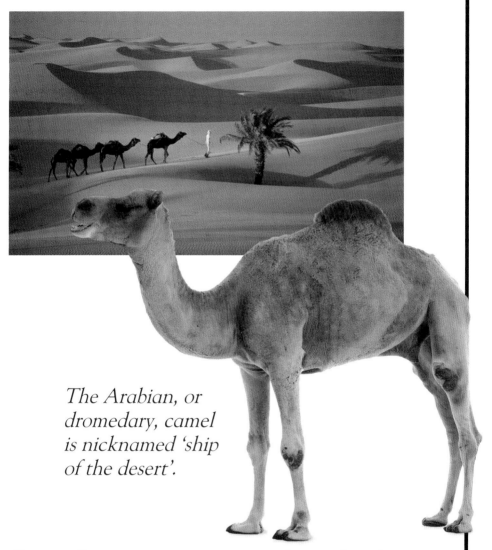

The Arabian, or dromedary, camel is nicknamed 'ship of the desert'.

Camels store water in their bodies so they can live more than five days in the desert without a drink.

Many creatures live in the ocean and cannot survive without water around them.
Some hunt or hide in deep water where it is cool and dark.
Others swim near the surface, searching for other animals to eat.

Gills

Fish have gills on the sides of their head so they can breathe underwater. They can't live out of water.

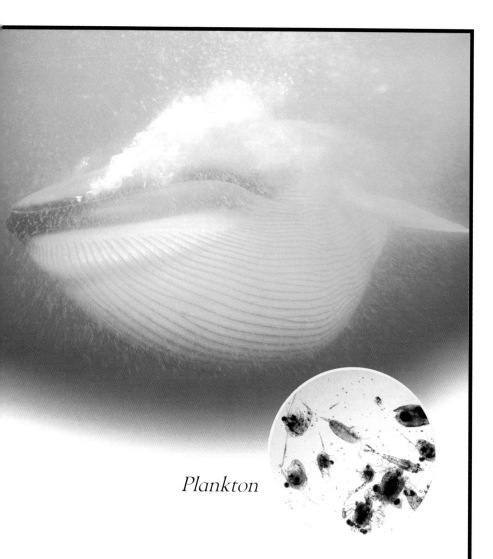

Plankton

Some whales, such as
the blue whale, eat millions
of tiny creatures called plankton.
These whales have long comblike
bristles instead of teeth.

Fish that live in rivers and lakes are called freshwater fish.
Many freshwater fish eat plants that grow in the water.
But some big fish, such as pike, eat smaller fish.

Many birds and animals live near water, where they find their food. They eat water plants, fish, insects or other animals.

Plants need water to grow.
Their roots push down
under the soil to find water.
They take in water
through their roots.

A cactus can grow
in the dry desert
because it stores
water for
a long time.

Rice is grown in countries
where there is a lot of rain.
This is because rice can only grow
in flooded fields.

In many places,
there is so much rain
that it causes floods.
People's homes get washed away.
In other places, there is sometimes
hardly any rain at all.
This is called drought.

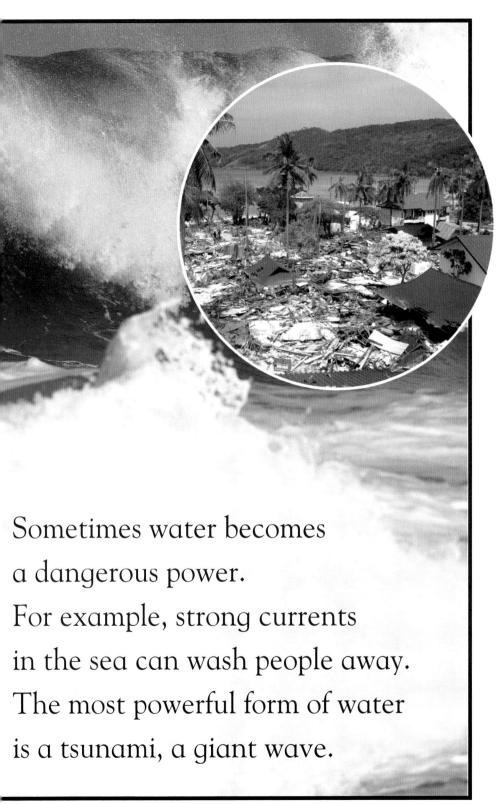

Sometimes water becomes
a dangerous power.
For example, strong currents
in the sea can wash people away.
The most powerful form of water
is a tsunami, a giant wave.

Water looks different when
it gets very cold or hot.

Liquid   *Solid*   *Gas*

The water we drink is liquid.
As water becomes very cold,
it freezes.
It becomes solid ice like
the frozen seas at the North Pole.
As water gets very hot, it becomes
steam and vanishes as a gas.

Steam

The steam from boiling kettles or steaming saucepans is dangerously hot and can burn you.

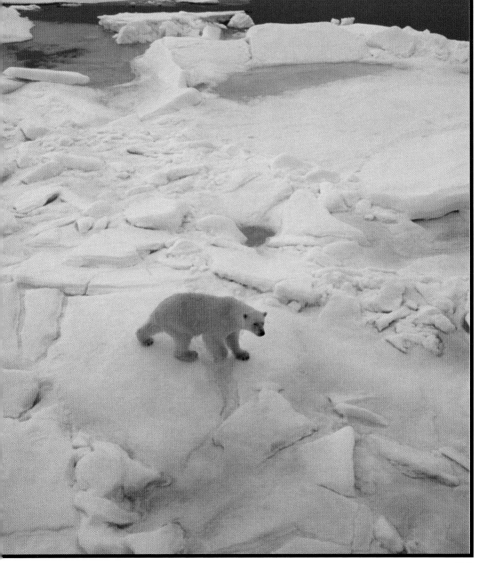

Water can be used to move
and power man-made machines.
The wheels and cogs of
a water mill are turned by water.
Rushing water is sometimes used
to make electricity.

The Rocket

One of the earliest steam engines was the Rocket. George Stephenson invented it in Britain in 1829.

Steam has been used
to power machines
for more than 250 years.
In a steam engine,
water is heated
in a large tank
to make steam.
The steam is used
to make the engine move.

It's important to keep
the world's water clean.
If a ship carrying oil crashes into
rocks, oil pours out into the sea
and harms the wildlife.

*Bird coated
in oil*

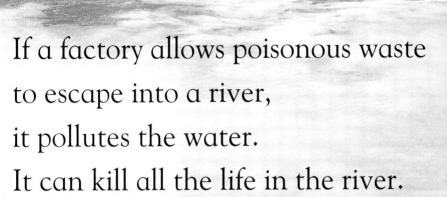

If a factory allows poisonous waste
to escape into a river,
it pollutes the water.
It can kill all the life in the river.

If children drink or play
in dirty water, they can catch
very dangerous diseases.

Many objects are absorbent.
This means that water
soaks into them.
If we go out in the rain,
our clothes absorb the water
and we feel wet.
Towels also absorb water
so they help us to get dry.

Many objects, such as umbrellas, are non-absorbent, so water does not soak into them.
They are especially useful for keeping off the rain!

Water is very important
to every living thing.
Without it no humans, or
animals or plants could exist
on this planet.

Scientists and astronauts
have been exploring other planets
for signs of water.
If they find water, it might mean
that life exists or used to exist
out there in space.

*NASA's Mars
Exploration
Rover*

Water Facts

Did you know that there is water in most things, including us? Our bodies are more than half water. Jellyfish are almost all water.

The longest river in the world is the Nile in Africa.

The deepest part of the oceans is the Mariana Trench in the Pacific Ocean.

The Caspian Sea is really a lake as there is land all around it. It is the biggest lake in the world.

Two-thirds of the water used in a home is used in the bathroom.

Today, at least 400 million people live in areas where there is not enough freshwater.